Check & Debit Card

REGISTER

If found please return to
Or call / email

Notes

Notes

Checking Account Ledger

Month: ____________________ Starting Balance: ____________________

	Date	Description	Ref	Debit (-)	Credit (+)	Balance
1						
2						
3						
4						
5						
6						
7						
8						
9						
10						
11						
12						
13						
14						
15						
16						
17						
18						
19						
20						
21						
22						
23						
24						

Notes

Checking Account Ledger

Month: ______________________ Starting Balance: ______________________

	Date	Description	Ref	Debit (-)	Credit (+)	Balance
1						
2						
3						
4						
5						
6						
7						
8						
9						
10						
11						
12						
13						
14						
15						
16						
17						
18						
19						
20						
21						
22						
23						
24						

Notes

Checking Account Ledger

Month: ______________________ Starting Balance: ______________________

	Date	Description	Ref	Debit (-)	Credit (+)	Balance
1						
2						
3						
4						
5						
6						
7						
8						
9						
10						
11						
12						
13						
14						
15						
16						
17						
18						
19						
20						
21						
22						
23						
24						

Notes

____

____

____

____

Checking Account Ledger

Month: ______________________ Starting Balance: ______________________

	Date	Description	Ref	Debit (-)	Credit (+)	Balance
1						
2						
3						
4						
5						
6						
7						
8						
9						
10						
11						
12						
13						
14						
15						
16						
17						
18						
19						
20						
21						
22						
23						
24						

Notes

Checking Account Ledger

Month: ______________________ Starting Balance: ______________________

	Date	Description	Ref	Debit (-)	Credit (+)	Balance
1						
2						
3						
4						
5						
6						
7						
8						
9						
10						
11						
12						
13						
14						
15						
16						
17						
18						
19						
20						
21						
22						
23						
24						

Notes

Checking Account Ledger

Month: ____________________ Starting Balance: ____________________

	Date	Description	Ref	Debit (-)	Credit (+)	Balance
1						
2						
3						
4						
5						
6						
7						
8						
9						
10						
11						
12						
13						
14						
15						
16						
17						
18						
19						
20						
21						
22						
23						
24						

Notes

Checking Account Ledger

Month: ____________________ Starting Balance: ____________________

	Date	Description	Ref	Debit (-)	Credit (+)	Balance
1						
2						
3						
4						
5						
6						
7						
8						
9						
10						
11						
12						
13						
14						
15						
16						
17						
18						
19						
20						
21						
22						
23						
24						

Notes

Checking Account Ledger

Month: ____________________ Starting Balance: ____________________

	Date	Description	Ref	Debit (-)	Credit (+)	Balance
1						
2						
3						
4						
5						
6						
7						
8						
9						
10						
11						
12						
13						
14						
15						
16						
17						
18						
19						
20						
21						
22						
23						
24						

Notes

Checking Account Ledger

Month: ______________________ Starting Balance: ______________________

	Date	Description	Ref	Debit (-)	Credit (+)	Balance
1						
2						
3						
4						
5						
6						
7						
8						
9						
10						
11						
12						
13						
14						
15						
16						
17						
18						
19						
20						
21						
22						
23						
24						

Notes

Checking Account Ledger

Month: ____________________ Starting Balance: ____________________

	Date	Description	Ref	Debit (-)	Credit (+)	Balance
1						
2						
3						
4						
5						
6						
7						
8						
9						
10						
11						
12						
13						
14						
15						
16						
17						
18						
19						
20						
21						
22						
23						
24						

Notes

Checking Account Ledger

Month: ____________________ Starting Balance: ____________________

	Date	Description	Ref	Debit (-)	Credit (+)	Balance
1						
2						
3						
4						
5						
6						
7						
8						
9						
10						
11						
12						
13						
14						
15						
16						
17						
18						
19						
20						
21						
22						
23						
24						

Notes

Checking Account Ledger

Month: ______________________ Starting Balance: ______________________

	Date	Description	Ref	Debit (-)	Credit (+)	Balance
1						
2						
3						
4						
5						
6						
7						
8						
9						
10						
11						
12						
13						
14						
15						
16						
17						
18						
19						
20						
21						
22						
23						
24						

Notes

Checking Account Ledger

Month: ______________________ Starting Balance: ______________________

	Date	Description	Ref	Debit (-)	Credit (+)	Balance
1						
2						
3						
4						
5						
6						
7						
8						
9						
10						
11						
12						
13						
14						
15						
16						
17						
18						
19						
20						
21						
22						
23						
24						

Notes

Checking Account Ledger

Month: ______________________ Starting Balance: ______________________

	Date	Description	Ref	Debit (-)	Credit (+)	Balance
1						
2						
3						
4						
5						
6						
7						
8						
9						
10						
11						
12						
13						
14						
15						
16						
17						
18						
19						
20						
21						
22						
23						
24						

Notes

Checking Account Ledger

Month: ____________________ Starting Balance: ____________________

	Date	Description	Ref	Debit (-)	Credit (+)	Balance
1						
2						
3						
4						
5						
6						
7						
8						
9						
10						
11						
12						
13						
14						
15						
16						
17						
18						
19						
20						
21						
22						
23						
24						

Notes

Checking Account Ledger

Month: ____________________ Starting Balance: ____________________

	Date	Description	Ref	Debit (-)	Credit (+)	Balance
1						
2						
3						
4						
5						
6						
7						
8						
9						
10						
11						
12						
13						
14						
15						
16						
17						
18						
19						
20						
21						
22						
23						
24						

Notes

Checking Account Ledger

Month: ______________________ Starting Balance: ______________________

	Date	Description	Ref	Debit (-)	Credit (+)	Balance
1						
2						
3						
4						
5						
6						
7						
8						
9						
10						
11						
12						
13						
14						
15						
16						
17						
18						
19						
20						
21						
22						
23						
24						

Notes

Checking Account Ledger

Month: ____________________ Starting Balance: ____________________

	Date	Description	Ref	Debit (-)	Credit (+)	Balance
1						
2						
3						
4						
5						
6						
7						
8						
9						
10						
11						
12						
13						
14						
15						
16						
17						
18						
19						
20						
21						
22						
23						
24						

Notes

Checking Account Ledger

Month: ______________________ Starting Balance: ______________________

	Date	Description	Ref	Debit (-)	Credit (+)	Balance
1						
2						
3						
4						
5						
6						
7						
8						
9						
10						
11						
12						
13						
14						
15						
16						
17						
18						
19						
20						
21						
22						
23						
24						

Notes

Checking Account Ledger

Month: ____________________ Starting Balance: ____________________

	Date	Description	Ref	Debit (-)	Credit (+)	Balance
1						
2						
3						
4						
5						
6						
7						
8						
9						
10						
11						
12						
13						
14						
15						
16						
17						
18						
19						
20						
21						
22						
23						
24						

Notes

Checking Account Ledger

Month: ______________________ Starting Balance: ______________________

	Date	Description	Ref	Debit (-)	Credit (+)	Balance
1						
2						
3						
4						
5						
6						
7						
8						
9						
10						
11						
12						
13						
14						
15						
16						
17						
18						
19						
20						
21						
22						
23						
24						

Notes

Checking Account Ledger

Month: ______________________ Starting Balance: ______________________

	Date	Description	Ref	Debit (-)	Credit (+)	Balance
1						
2						
3						
4						
5						
6						
7						
8						
9						
10						
11						
12						
13						
14						
15						
16						
17						
18						
19						
20						
21						
22						
23						
24						

Notes

Checking Account Ledger

Month: ______________________ Starting Balance: ______________________

	Date	Description	Ref	Debit (-)	Credit (+)	Balance
1						
2						
3						
4						
5						
6						
7						
8						
9						
10						
11						
12						
13						
14						
15						
16						
17						
18						
19						
20						
21						
22						
23						
24						

Notes

Checking Account Ledger

Month: ______________________ Starting Balance: ______________________

	Date	Description	Ref	Debit (-)	Credit (+)	Balance
1						
2						
3						
4						
5						
6						
7						
8						
9						
10						
11						
12						
13						
14						
15						
16						
17						
18						
19						
20						
21						
22						
23						
24						

Notes

____

____

____

____

Checking Account Ledger

Month: ____________________ Starting Balance: ____________________

	Date	Description	Ref	Debit (-)	Credit (+)	Balance
1						
2						
3						
4						
5						
6						
7						
8						
9						
10						
11						
12						
13						
14						
15						
16						
17						
18						
19						
20						
21						
22						
23						
24						

Notes

Checking Account Ledger

Month: ______________________ Starting Balance: ______________________

	Date	Description	Ref	Debit (-)	Credit (+)	Balance
1						
2						
3						
4						
5						
6						
7						
8						
9						
10						
11						
12						
13						
14						
15						
16						
17						
18						
19						
20						
21						
22						
23						
24						

Notes

Checking Account Ledger

Month: ____________________ Starting Balance: ____________________

	Date	Description	Ref	Debit (-)	Credit (+)	Balance
1						
2						
3						
4						
5						
6						
7						
8						
9						
10						
11						
12						
13						
14						
15						
16						
17						
18						
19						
20						
21						
22						
23						
24						

Notes

Checking Account Ledger

Month: ____________________ Starting Balance: ____________________

	Date	Description	Ref	Debit (-)	Credit (+)	Balance
1						
2						
3						
4						
5						
6						
7						
8						
9						
10						
11						
12						
13						
14						
15						
16						
17						
18						
19						
20						
21						
22						
23						
24						

Notes

Checking Account Ledger

Month: ______________________ Starting Balance: ______________________

	Date	Description	Ref	Debit (-)	Credit (+)	Balance
1						
2						
3						
4						
5						
6						
7						
8						
9						
10						
11						
12						
13						
14						
15						
16						
17						
18						
19						
20						
21						
22						
23						
24						

Notes

Checking Account Ledger

Month: ____________________ Starting Balance: ____________________

	Date	Description	Ref	Debit (-)		Credit (+)		Balance	
1									
2									
3									
4									
5									
6									
7									
8									
9									
10									
11									
12									
13									
14									
15									
16									
17									
18									
19									
20									
21									
22									
23									
24									

Notes

Checking Account Ledger

Month: ______________________ Starting Balance: ______________________

	Date	Description	Ref	Debit (-)	Credit (+)	Balance
1						
2						
3						
4						
5						
6						
7						
8						
9						
10						
11						
12						
13						
14						
15						
16						
17						
18						
19						
20						
21						
22						
23						
24						

Notes

Checking Account Ledger

Month: ____________________ Starting Balance: ____________________

	Date	Description	Ref	Debit (-)	Credit (+)	Balance
1						
2						
3						
4						
5						
6						
7						
8						
9						
10						
11						
12						
13						
14						
15						
16						
17						
18						
19						
20						
21						
22						
23						
24						

Notes

Checking Account Ledger

Month: ____________________ Starting Balance: ____________________

	Date	Description	Ref	Debit (-)	Credit (+)	Balance
1						
2						
3						
4						
5						
6						
7						
8						
9						
10						
11						
12						
13						
14						
15						
16						
17						
18						
19						
20						
21						
22						
23						
24						

Notes

Checking Account Ledger

Month: ______________________ Starting Balance: ______________________

	Date	Description	Ref	Debit (-)	Credit (+)	Balance
1						
2						
3						
4						
5						
6						
7						
8						
9						
10						
11						
12						
13						
14						
15						
16						
17						
18						
19						
20						
21						
22						
23						
24						

Notes

Checking Account Ledger

Month: ______________________ Starting Balance: ______________________

	Date	Description	Ref	Debit (-)	Credit (+)	Balance
1						
2						
3						
4						
5						
6						
7						
8						
9						
10						
11						
12						
13						
14						
15						
16						
17						
18						
19						
20						
21						
22						
23						
24						

Notes

Checking Account Ledger

Month: ______________________ Starting Balance: ______________________

	Date	Description	Ref	Debit (-)	Credit (+)	Balance
1						
2						
3						
4						
5						
6						
7						
8						
9						
10						
11						
12						
13						
14						
15						
16						
17						
18						
19						
20						
21						
22						
23						
24						

Notes

Checking Account Ledger

Month: ____________________ Starting Balance: ____________________

	Date	Description	Ref	Debit (-)	Credit (+)	Balance
1						
2						
3						
4						
5						
6						
7						
8						
9						
10						
11						
12						
13						
14						
15						
16						
17						
18						
19						
20						
21						
22						
23						
24						

Notes

Checking Account Ledger

Month: ______________________ Starting Balance: ______________________

	Date	Description	Ref	Debit (-)	Credit (+)	Balance
1						
2						
3						
4						
5						
6						
7						
8						
9						
10						
11						
12						
13						
14						
15						
16						
17						
18						
19						
20						
21						
22						
23						
24						

Notes

Checking Account Ledger

Month: ____________________ Starting Balance: ______________________________

	Date	Description	Ref	Debit (-)	Credit (+)	Balance
1						
2						
3						
4						
5						
6						
7						
8						
9						
10						
11						
12						
13						
14						
15						
16						
17						
18						
19						
20						
21						
22						
23						
24						

Notes

Checking Account Ledger

Month: ____________________ Starting Balance: ____________________

	Date	Description	Ref	Debit (-)	Credit (+)	Balance
1						
2						
3						
4						
5						
6						
7						
8						
9						
10						
11						
12						
13						
14						
15						
16						
17						
18						
19						
20						
21						
22						
23						
24						

Notes

Checking Account Ledger

Month: ______________________ Starting Balance: ______________________

	Date	Description	Ref	Debit (-)	Credit (+)	Balance
1						
2						
3						
4						
5						
6						
7						
8						
9						
10						
11						
12						
13						
14						
15						
16						
17						
18						
19						
20						
21						
22						
23						
24						

Notes

Checking Account Ledger

Month: ______________________ Starting Balance: ______________________

	Date	Description	Ref	Debit (-)	Credit (+)	Balance
1						
2						
3						
4						
5						
6						
7						
8						
9						
10						
11						
12						
13						
14						
15						
16						
17						
18						
19						
20						
21						
22						
23						
24						

Notes

Checking Account Ledger

Month: ____________________ Starting Balance: ______________________________

	Date	Description	Ref	Debit (-)	Credit (+)	Balance
1						
2						
3						
4						
5						
6						
7						
8						
9						
10						
11						
12						
13						
14						
15						
16						
17						
18						
19						
20						
21						
22						
23						
24						

Notes

Checking Account Ledger

Month: ______________________ Starting Balance: ______________________

	Date	Description	Ref	Debit (-)	Credit (+)	Balance
1						
2						
3						
4						
5						
6						
7						
8						
9						
10						
11						
12						
13						
14						
15						
16						
17						
18						
19						
20						
21						
22						
23						
24						

Notes

Checking Account Ledger

Month: ____________________ Starting Balance: ____________________

	Date	Description	Ref	Debit (-)	Credit (+)	Balance
1						
2						
3						
4						
5						
6						
7						
8						
9						
10						
11						
12						
13						
14						
15						
16						
17						
18						
19						
20						
21						
22						
23						
24						

Notes

Checking Account Ledger

Month: ______________________ Starting Balance: ______________________

	Date	Description	Ref	Debit (-)	Credit (+)	Balance
1						
2						
3						
4						
5						
6						
7						
8						
9						
10						
11						
12						
13						
14						
15						
16						
17						
18						
19						
20						
21						
22						
23						
24						

Notes

Checking Account Ledger

Month: ______________________ Starting Balance: ______________________

	Date	Description	Ref	Debit (-)	Credit (+)	Balance
1						
2						
3						
4						
5						
6						
7						
8						
9						
10						
11						
12						
13						
14						
15						
16						
17						
18						
19						
20						
21						
22						
23						
24						

Notes

Checking Account Ledger

Month: ______________________ Starting Balance: ______________________

	Date	Description	Ref	Debit (-)	Credit (+)	Balance
1						
2						
3						
4						
5						
6						
7						
8						
9						
10						
11						
12						
13						
14						
15						
16						
17						
18						
19						
20						
21						
22						
23						
24						

Notes

Checking Account Ledger

Month: ____________________ Starting Balance: ____________________

	Date	Description	Ref	Debit (-)	Credit (+)	Balance
1						
2						
3						
4						
5						
6						
7						
8						
9						
10						
11						
12						
13						
14						
15						
16						
17						
18						
19						
20						
21						
22						
23						
24						

Notes

Checking Account Ledger

Month: ______________________ Starting Balance: ______________________

	Date	Description	Ref	Debit (-)	Credit (+)	Balance
1						
2						
3						
4						
5						
6						
7						
8						
9						
10						
11						
12						
13						
14						
15						
16						
17						
18						
19						
20						
21						
22						
23						
24						

Notes

Checking Account Ledger

Month: ______________________ Starting Balance: ______________________

	Date	Description	Ref	Debit (-)	Credit (+)	Balance
1						
2						
3						
4						
5						
6						
7						
8						
9						
10						
11						
12						
13						
14						
15						
16						
17						
18						
19						
20						
21						
22						
23						
24						

Notes

Checking Account Ledger

Month: ______________________ Starting Balance: ______________________

	Date	Description	Ref	Debit (-)	Credit (+)	Balance
1						
2						
3						
4						
5						
6						
7						
8						
9						
10						
11						
12						
13						
14						
15						
16						
17						
18						
19						
20						
21						
22						
23						
24						

Notes

Checking Account Ledger

Month: ____________________ Starting Balance: ____________________

	Date	Description	Ref	Debit (-)	Credit (+)	Balance
1						
2						
3						
4						
5						
6						
7						
8						
9						
10						
11						
12						
13						
14						
15						
16						
17						
18						
19						
20						
21						
22						
23						
24						

Notes

Checking Account Ledger

Month: ____________________ Starting Balance: ____________________

	Date	Description	Ref	Debit (-)	Credit (+)	Balance
1						
2						
3						
4						
5						
6						
7						
8						
9						
10						
11						
12						
13						
14						
15						
16						
17						
18						
19						
20						
21						
22						
23						
24						

Notes

Checking Account Ledger

Month: ____________________ Starting Balance: ____________________

	Date	Description	Ref	Debit (-)	Credit (+)	Balance
1						
2						
3						
4						
5						
6						
7						
8						
9						
10						
11						
12						
13						
14						
15						
16						
17						
18						
19						
20						
21						
22						
23						
24						

Notes

Checking Account Ledger

Month: ______________________ Starting Balance: ______________________

	Date	Description	Ref	Debit (-)	Credit (+)	Balance
1						
2						
3						
4						
5						
6						
7						
8						
9						
10						
11						
12						
13						
14						
15						
16						
17						
18						
19						
20						
21						
22						
23						
24						

Notes

Checking Account Ledger

Month: ____________________ Starting Balance: ____________________

	Date	Description	Ref	Debit (-)	Credit (+)	Balance
1						
2						
3						
4						
5						
6						
7						
8						
9						
10						
11						
12						
13						
14						
15						
16						
17						
18						
19						
20						
21						
22						
23						
24						

Notes

Checking Account Ledger

Month: ______________________ Starting Balance: ______________________

	Date	Description	Ref	Debit (-)	Credit (+)	Balance
1						
2						
3						
4						
5						
6						
7						
8						
9						
10						
11						
12						
13						
14						
15						
16						
17						
18						
19						
20						
21						
22						
23						
24						

Notes

Checking Account Ledger

Month: ______________________ Starting Balance: ______________________

	Date	Description	Ref	Debit (-)	Credit (+)	Balance
1						
2						
3						
4						
5						
6						
7						
8						
9						
10						
11						
12						
13						
14						
15						
16						
17						
18						
19						
20						
21						
22						
23						
24						

Notes

Checking Account Ledger

Month: ______________________ Starting Balance: ______________________

	Date	Description	Ref	Debit (-)	Credit (+)	Balance
1						
2						
3						
4						
5						
6						
7						
8						
9						
10						
11						
12						
13						
14						
15						
16						
17						
18						
19						
20						
21						
22						
23						
24						

Notes

Checking Account Ledger

Month: ______________________ Starting Balance: ______________________

	Date	Description	Ref	Debit (-)	Credit (+)	Balance
1						
2						
3						
4						
5						
6						
7						
8						
9						
10						
11						
12						
13						
14						
15						
16						
17						
18						
19						
20						
21						
22						
23						
24						

Notes

Checking Account Ledger

Month: ______________________ Starting Balance: ______________________

	Date	Description	Ref	Debit (-)	Credit (+)	Balance
1						
2						
3						
4						
5						
6						
7						
8						
9						
10						
11						
12						
13						
14						
15						
16						
17						
18						
19						
20						
21						
22						
23						
24						

Notes

Checking Account Ledger

Month: ____________________ Starting Balance: ____________________

	Date	Description	Ref	Debit (-)	Credit (+)	Balance
1						
2						
3						
4						
5						
6						
7						
8						
9						
10						
11						
12						
13						
14						
15						
16						
17						
18						
19						
20						
21						
22						
23						
24						

Notes

Checking Account Ledger

Month: ______________________ Starting Balance: ______________________

	Date	Description	Ref	Debit (-)	Credit (+)	Balance
1						
2						
3						
4						
5						
6						
7						
8						
9						
10						
11						
12						
13						
14						
15						
16						
17						
18						
19						
20						
21						
22						
23						
24						

Notes

Checking Account Ledger

Month: ______________________ Starting Balance: ______________________

	Date	Description	Ref	Debit (-)	Credit (+)	Balance
1						
2						
3						
4						
5						
6						
7						
8						
9						
10						
11						
12						
13						
14						
15						
16						
17						
18						
19						
20						
21						
22						
23						
24						

Notes

Checking Account Ledger

Month: ______________________ Starting Balance: ______________________

	Date	Description	Ref	Debit (-)	Credit (+)	Balance
1						
2						
3						
4						
5						
6						
7						
8						
9						
10						
11						
12						
13						
14						
15						
16						
17						
18						
19						
20						
21						
22						
23						
24						

Notes

Checking Account Ledger

Month: ____________________ Starting Balance: ____________________

	Date	Description	Ref	Debit (-)	Credit (+)	Balance
1						
2						
3						
4						
5						
6						
7						
8						
9						
10						
11						
12						
13						
14						
15						
16						
17						
18						
19						
20						
21						
22						
23						
24						

Notes

Checking Account Ledger

Month: ____________________ Starting Balance: ____________________

	Date	Description	Ref	Debit (-)	Credit (+)	Balance
1						
2						
3						
4						
5						
6						
7						
8						
9						
10						
11						
12						
13						
14						
15						
16						
17						
18						
19						
20						
21						
22						
23						
24						

Notes

Checking Account Ledger

Month: ______________________ Starting Balance: ______________________

	Date	Description	Ref	Debit (-)	Credit (+)	Balance
1						
2						
3						
4						
5						
6						
7						
8						
9						
10						
11						
12						
13						
14						
15						
16						
17						
18						
19						
20						
21						
22						
23						
24						

Notes

Checking Account Ledger

Month: ____________________ Starting Balance: ____________________

	Date	Description	Ref	Debit (-)	Credit (+)	Balance
1						
2						
3						
4						
5						
6						
7						
8						
9						
10						
11						
12						
13						
14						
15						
16						
17						
18						
19						
20						
21						
22						
23						
24						

Notes

Checking Account Ledger

Month: ______________________ Starting Balance: ______________________

	Date	Description	Ref	Debit (-)	Credit (+)	Balance
1						
2						
3						
4						
5						
6						
7						
8						
9						
10						
11						
12						
13						
14						
15						
16						
17						
18						
19						
20						
21						
22						
23						
24						

Notes

Checking Account Ledger

Month: ______________________ Starting Balance: ______________________

	Date	Description	Ref	Debit (-)	Credit (+)	Balance
1						
2						
3						
4						
5						
6						
7						
8						
9						
10						
11						
12						
13						
14						
15						
16						
17						
18						
19						
20						
21						
22						
23						
24						

Notes

Checking Account Ledger

Month: ______________________ Starting Balance: ______________________

	Date	Description	Ref	Debit (-)	Credit (+)	Balance
1						
2						
3						
4						
5						
6						
7						
8						
9						
10						
11						
12						
13						
14						
15						
16						
17						
18						
19						
20						
21						
22						
23						
24						

Notes

Checking Account Ledger

Month: ____________________ Starting Balance: ____________________

	Date	Description	Ref	Debit (-)		Credit (+)		Balance	
1									
2									
3									
4									
5									
6									
7									
8									
9									
10									
11									
12									
13									
14									
15									
16									
17									
18									
19									
20									
21									
22									
23									
24									

Notes

Checking Account Ledger

Month: ______________________ Starting Balance: ______________________

	Date	Description	Ref	Debit (-)	Credit (+)	Balance
1						
2						
3						
4						
5						
6						
7						
8						
9						
10						
11						
12						
13						
14						
15						
16						
17						
18						
19						
20						
21						
22						
23						
24						

Notes

Checking Account Ledger

Month: ______________________ Starting Balance: ______________________

	Date	Description	Ref	Debit (-)	Credit (+)	Balance
1						
2						
3						
4						
5						
6						
7						
8						
9						
10						
11						
12						
13						
14						
15						
16						
17						
18						
19						
20						
21						
22						
23						
24						

Notes

Checking Account Ledger

Month: ______________________ Starting Balance: ______________________

	Date	Description	Ref	Debit (-)	Credit (+)	Balance
1						
2						
3						
4						
5						
6						
7						
8						
9						
10						
11						
12						
13						
14						
15						
16						
17						
18						
19						
20						
21						
22						
23						
24						

Notes

Checking Account Ledger

Month: ______________________ Starting Balance: ______________________

	Date	Description	Ref	Debit (-)		Credit (+)		Balance	
1									
2									
3									
4									
5									
6									
7									
8									
9									
10									
11									
12									
13									
14									
15									
16									
17									
18									
19									
20									
21									
22									
23									
24									

Notes

Checking Account Ledger

Month: ______________________ Starting Balance: ______________________

	Date	Description	Ref	Debit (-)	Credit (+)	Balance
1						
2						
3						
4						
5						
6						
7						
8						
9						
10						
11						
12						
13						
14						
15						
16						
17						
18						
19						
20						
21						
22						
23						
24						

Notes

Checking Account Ledger

Month: ______________________ Starting Balance: ______________________

	Date	Description	Ref	Debit (-)	Credit (+)	Balance
1						
2						
3						
4						
5						
6						
7						
8						
9						
10						
11						
12						
13						
14						
15						
16						
17						
18						
19						
20						
21						
22						
23						
24						

Notes

Checking Account Ledger

Month: ______________ Starting Balance: ______________

	Date	Description	Ref	Debit (-)	Credit (+)	Balance
1						
2						
3						
4						
5						
6						
7						
8						
9						
10						
11						
12						
13						
14						
15						
16						
17						
18						
19						
20						
21						
22						
23						
24						

Notes

Checking Account Ledger

Month: ______________________ Starting Balance: ______________________

	Date	Description	Ref	Debit (-)	Credit (+)	Balance
1						
2						
3						
4						
5						
6						
7						
8						
9						
10						
11						
12						
13						
14						
15						
16						
17						
18						
19						
20						
21						
22						
23						
24						

Notes

____

____

____

____

Checking Account Ledger

Month: ______________________ Starting Balance: ______________________

	Date	Description	Ref	Debit (-)	Credit (+)	Balance
1						
2						
3						
4						
5						
6						
7						
8						
9						
10						
11						
12						
13						
14						
15						
16						
17						
18						
19						
20						
21						
22						
23						
24						

Notes

Checking Account Ledger

Month: ____________________ Starting Balance: ______________________________

	Date	Description	Ref	Debit (-)	Credit (+)	Balance
1						
2						
3						
4						
5						
6						
7						
8						
9						
10						
11						
12						
13						
14						
15						
16						
17						
18						
19						
20						
21						
22						
23						
24						

Notes

Checking Account Ledger

Month: ____________________ Starting Balance: ____________________

	Date	Description	Ref	Debit (-)	Credit (+)	Balance
1						
2						
3						
4						
5						
6						
7						
8						
9						
10						
11						
12						
13						
14						
15						
16						
17						
18						
19						
20						
21						
22						
23						
24						

Notes

Checking Account Ledger

Month: ____________________ Starting Balance: ____________________

	Date	Description	Ref	Debit (-)	Credit (+)	Balance
1						
2						
3						
4						
5						
6						
7						
8						
9						
10						
11						
12						
13						
14						
15						
16						
17						
18						
19						
20						
21						
22						
23						
24						

Notes

Checking Account Ledger

Month: ____________________ Starting Balance: ____________________

	Date	Description	Ref	Debit (-)	Credit (+)	Balance
1						
2						
3						
4						
5						
6						
7						
8						
9						
10						
11						
12						
13						
14						
15						
16						
17						
18						
19						
20						
21						
22						
23						
24						

Notes

Checking Account Ledger

Month: ____________________ Starting Balance: ____________________

	Date	Description	Ref	Debit (-)	Credit (+)	Balance
1						
2						
3						
4						
5						
6						
7						
8						
9						
10						
11						
12						
13						
14						
15						
16						
17						
18						
19						
20						
21						
22						
23						
24						

Notes

Checking Account Ledger

Month: ____________ Starting Balance: ____________

	Date	Description	Ref	Debit (-)	Credit (+)	Balance
1						
2						
3						
4						
5						
6						
7						
8						
9						
10						
11						
12						
13						
14						
15						
16						
17						
18						
19						
20						
21						
22						
23						
24						

Notes

Checking Account Ledger

Month: ____________________ Starting Balance: ____________________

	Date	Description	Ref	Debit (-)	Credit (+)	Balance
1						
2						
3						
4						
5						
6						
7						
8						
9						
10						
11						
12						
13						
14						
15						
16						
17						
18						
19						
20						
21						
22						
23						
24						

Notes

Checking Account Ledger

Month: ______________________ Starting Balance: ______________________

	Date	Description	Ref	Debit (-)	Credit (+)	Balance
1						
2						
3						
4						
5						
6						
7						
8						
9						
10						
11						
12						
13						
14						
15						
16						
17						
18						
19						
20						
21						
22						
23						
24						

Notes

Checking Account Ledger

Month: ______________________ Starting Balance: ______________________

	Date	Description	Ref	Debit (-)	Credit (+)	Balance
1						
2						
3						
4						
5						
6						
7						
8						
9						
10						
11						
12						
13						
14						
15						
16						
17						
18						
19						
20						
21						
22						
23						
24						

Notes

Checking Account Ledger

Month: ______________________ Starting Balance: ______________________

	Date	Description	Ref	Debit (-)	Credit (+)	Balance
1						
2						
3						
4						
5						
6						
7						
8						
9						
10						
11						
12						
13						
14						
15						
16						
17						
18						
19						
20						
21						
22						
23						
24						

Notes

Checking Account Ledger

Month: ____________________ Starting Balance: ______________________________

	Date	Description	Ref	Debit (-)	Credit (+)	Balance
1						
2						
3						
4						
5						
6						
7						
8						
9						
10						
11						
12						
13						
14						
15						
16						
17						
18						
19						
20						
21						
22						
23						
24						

Notes

Checking Account Ledger

Month: ____________________ Starting Balance: ____________________

	Date	Description	Ref	Debit (-)	Credit (+)	Balance
1						
2						
3						
4						
5						
6						
7						
8						
9						
10						
11						
12						
13						
14						
15						
16						
17						
18						
19						
20						
21						
22						
23						
24						

Notes

Checking Account Ledger

Month: ____________________ Starting Balance: ______________________________

	Date	Description	Ref	Debit (-)	Credit (+)	Balance
1						
2						
3						
4						
5						
6						
7						
8						
9						
10						
11						
12						
13						
14						
15						
16						
17						
18						
19						
20						
21						
22						
23						
24						

Notes

Checking Account Ledger

Month: ____________________ Starting Balance: ____________________

	Date	Description	Ref	Debit (-)	Credit (+)	Balance
1						
2						
3						
4						
5						
6						
7						
8						
9						
10						
11						
12						
13						
14						
15						
16						
17						
18						
19						
20						
21						
22						
23						
24						

Notes

Checking Account Ledger

Month: ____________________ Starting Balance: ____________________

	Date	Description	Ref	Debit (-)	Credit (+)	Balance
1						
2						
3						
4						
5						
6						
7						
8						
9						
10						
11						
12						
13						
14						
15						
16						
17						
18						
19						
20						
21						
22						
23						
24						

Notes

Checking Account Ledger

Month: ____________________ Starting Balance: ____________________

	Date	Description	Ref	Debit (-)	Credit (+)	Balance
1						
2						
3						
4						
5						
6						
7						
8						
9						
10						
11						
12						
13						
14						
15						
16						
17						
18						
19						
20						
21						
22						
23						
24						

Notes

Checking Account Ledger

Month: ______________________ Starting Balance: ______________________

	Date	Description	Ref	Debit (-)	Credit (+)	Balance
1						
2						
3						
4						
5						
6						
7						
8						
9						
10						
11						
12						
13						
14						
15						
16						
17						
18						
19						
20						
21						
22						
23						
24						

Notes

____

____

____

____

Printed in the USA
CPSIA information can be obtained
at www.ICGtesting.com
LVHW052244270923
759571LV00014BA/473

9 781710 485721